YOU CHOO BOOKS

Life as a Knight

An Interactive History Adventure

by Rachael Hanel

Consultant:
Phillip C. Adamo
Associate Professor and Chair of History
Director of Medieval Studies
Augsburg College
Minneapolis, Minnesota

CAPSTONE PRESS
a capstone imprint

You Choose Books are published by Capstone Press,
1710 Roe Crest Drive, North Mankato, Minnesota 56003.
www.capstonepub.com

Library of Congress Cataloging-in-Publication Data
Hanel, Rachael.
   Life as a knight: an interactive history adventure / by Rachael Hanel.
   p. cm. — (You choose — warriors)
   Includes bibliographical references and index.
   Summary: "Describes the lives of knights in medieval Europe. The reader's choices reveal
historical details from the perspectives of a French knight during the Crusades, an English knight
during the Hundred Years' War, and a German knight during the Peasants' War" — Provided
by publisher.
   ISBN 978-1-4296-4026-8 (lib. bdg.)
   ISBN 978-1-4296-4866-0 (paperback)
   1. Knights and knighthood — Juvenile literature. 2. Civilization, Medieval — Juvenile
literature. I. Title. II. Series.
CR4513.H38 2010
940.1 — dc22
                                       2009032952

Editorial Credits
Angie Kaelberer, editor; Veronica Bianchini, designer; Wanda Winch, media researcher;
   Laura Manthe, production specialist

Photo Credits
akg-images: 15, 88, 92, Collection Archiv F. Kunst & Geschichte, 79, Max Lingner, The German
Peasants War, 98; The Bridgeman Art Library: ©British Library Board, All Rights Reserved/
British Library, London, UK, 64, ©Look and Learn/Private Collection 6, 56, 69, Jackson,
Peter, 59, McBride, Angus, 72, DHM/Deutsches Historisches Museum, Berlin, Germany, 83,
Manchester Art Gallery, UK, Gilbert, John, 36, The Stapleton Collection/Private Collection, 28;
Getty Images Inc.: Photographer's Choice/Colin Anderson, cover, The Bridgeman Art Library/
Titan, 76; iStockphoto: duncan1890, 27; Mary Evans Picture Library: 10, Douglas McCarthy,
100; North Wind Picture Archives: 32; Peter Newark's Pictures: 23, 40, 46, 50, 52, 66, 104

Printed in China.
122014   008687R

TABLE OF CONTENTS

ABOUT YOUR ADVENTURE

YOU are a knight during the Middle Ages. You've sworn to fight fairly and protect the helpless. What kinds of adventures await you?

In this book, you'll explore how the choices people made meant the difference between life and death. The events you'll experience happened to real people.

Chapter One sets the scene. Then you choose which path to read. Follow the directions at the bottom of each page. The choices you make will change your outcome. After you finish one path, go back and read the others for new perspectives and more adventures.

YOU CHOOSE the path
you take through history.

Sturdy warhorses carried medieval knights into battle.

Courage, Bravery, and Honor

With blazing speed, your trusty hunting horse carries you into your village. At the stable, you dismount and give your horse a pat. "Good boy," you say. "You rest now. I need you to always be at your strongest."

A knight's horses are his most valuable possessions. A well-trained hunting horse helps you provide food for yourself and others. Without a strong riding horse, you would have no way to travel easily around the countryside. And without a warhorse, you would be useless in battle.

Turn the page.

As a knight, you are greatly admired. You have been chosen for your strength, bravery, and intelligence. You serve a noble class of earls, lords, and kings. If the nobles need to fight to protect their land and wealth, they call on you to help.

When you're not in battle, you look after your manor, which includes a village and the land surrounding it. You watch over the serfs, who farm the land. You collect taxes from them in the form of food. Some you give to your lord. You keep the rest to take care of your family.

Knights are held to high standards. At all times, you should act with courtesy and politeness. Knights call this chivalry. Under the code of chivalry, you are not to lie, cheat, or steal. Even on the battlefield, you are to honor and respect your opponents. Of course, not all knights live by this code, but you try always to follow it.

A knight's life is not without danger. On the battlefield, you are open to attack. Swords and arrows can pierce armor and metal mesh clothing, which is called mail. At home, you must be on guard against attacks on your village. Even jousting tournaments and melees, which are supposed to be fun, can turn dangerous or deadly.

But you can make choices that will affect the outcome of your life. As a knight, you have a chance to take part in some of history's most remarkable events. Your actions will be remembered for centuries to come.

↠ To be a French knight in 1096, turn to page **11**.

↠ To be an English knight in 1346, turn to page **41**.

↠ To be a German knight in 1525, turn to page **73**.

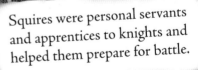

Squires were personal servants and apprentices to knights and helped them prepare for battle.

CHAPTER 2

The Battle for the Holy Land

It's early in the spring of 1096. You've just returned home after a ride through the French countryside. You put your horse into the stable and head toward the large stone house. This is Lord Humbert's estate, where you live as a squire.

You think about when you first arrived at the estate as a 7-year-old page. You and the other pages attended school. You played wrestling games and practiced fighting with wooden swords called wasters.

Turn the page.

But now that you're a squire, the training is more serious. You study with skilled knights. They show you how to powerfully thrust lances and swords. You spend days riding horses and training them. You also learn about manners and the proper way to carve meat at your lord's table.

Suddenly, you hear a loud noise. You race to the house to see what's going on. "The neighboring village has been attacked!" the lord's steward shouts, breathless from running. "All knights must ride to the village. If this attack is not stopped, our village might be next."

Lords often attack other lords' villages, hoping to gain more land and power. This is the first attack you've seen.

You grab your lance and start for the stable. The steward stops you.

"Where do you think you're going?" he asks. "You are not yet a knight. You must stay behind."

"But . . ."

"We have plenty of knights. They can take care of this. You are needed here. The squires must be on guard in case of a surprise attack."

You understand, but you're disappointed. Then you realize that you could sneak into the battle.

→ To protect the village, turn to page **14**.

→ To sneak into the battle, turn to page **30**.

You watch the knights ride off into the distance. It's a beautiful sight. The sleek horses are strong and fast. The metal links of the knights' mail shirts glint in the sun. Someday you will also get to ride into battle.

You patrol the outer limits of the village with the other squires. But thankfully, the enemy stays away.

After a few days, the lord's men return. "It was a tough fight, but we won," Lord Humbert says. "Unfortunately, we lost several men."

Later that evening, the lord gathers you and the other squires together.

"I need more fighting men to replace those who have been killed or injured," he says. "It is time for the knighting ceremony. You all have earned this honor."

Most knighting ceremonies of the time took place in churches.

The next morning, you enter the village church. You kneel with the other squires in front of the priest. The priest walks down the line and finally stands before you. He taps you on the shoulder with a sword. You are now a knight.

Lord Humbert tucks your sword into a belt. He buckles the belt around your waist. He also gives you a new pair of spurs. You receive a village to oversee. You also receive a house and land for your use for as long as you serve Lord Humbert.

Turn the page.

A few days later, several of the other new knights visit you. "Knights from other villages are planning a melee," one says to you. "Will you come with us?"

During a melee, groups of knights from several villages gather together and practice their fighting skills. Two knights fight until one is knocked off his horse or hurt. A knight who is knocked off his horse must give his horse and armor to his opponent. It would be a great way to show off your skills and maybe win some equipment. But it's also time for the serfs to plant the crops. You should be there during planting to supervise them.

→ To participate in the melee, go to page **17**.

→ To attend to your property, turn to page **18**.

At the melee, you look around for an opponent. You walk over to your friend Robert, who also serves Lord Humbert.

"Pierre, a knight from the neighboring village, wants to be your opponent in this round," Robert says. "You also have a challenge from another knight. His name is Jeffrey, and he's tough. He likes to pick on the younger knights to show his strength. His horse and equipment are better than those of any other knight here."

It can take years to buy the best equipment and horses. If you can unseat Jeffrey from his horse, you would walk away a rich young man. But you're not sure about facing such a powerful opponent in your first melee.

➤ *To fight Pierre, turn to page* **20**.

➤ *To fight Jeffrey, turn to page* **32**.

Knighthood comes with responsibilities. Crops must be planted in the spring and harvested in the fall. Villagers come to you to settle disputes. If you carefully attend to your property and the village, you can start to gain wealth.

One day, some fellow knights visit you in your home.

"Have you heard about the pope's sermon at Clermont?" Sir Bernard asks. You shake your head.

Bernard continues. "Pope Urban II has warned us of the problems in the Holy Land. When Christian pilgrims travel there, they are harassed and sometimes killed by the Muslims who live there. The pope wants every able-bodied man to go there and take the Holy Land from the Muslims. We're going. Will you come with us?"

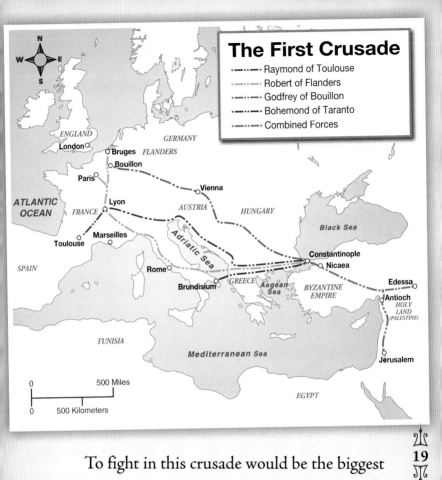

The First Crusade

- ·····- Raymond of Toulouse
- ·····- Robert of Flanders
- ·····- Godfrey of Bouillon
- ·····- Bohemond of Taranto
- ·····- Combined Forces

To fight in this crusade would be the biggest adventure of your life. But what about your village? A village with few men is at risk of attack by outlaws and people from other villages.

➤ To stay behind, turn to page 22.

➤ To fight in the crusade, turn to page 23.

You square off with Pierre. You don't manage to unseat him from his horse, but he doesn't knock you off your horse either. You don't win anything, but you're glad to have the chance to practice your skills.

A few days later, Lord Humbert gathers his knights together. "We've received an important message from Pope Urban II," he says. "He has declared war in the Holy Land. Muslims are attacking Christian pilgrims who travel to Jerusalem. The pope wants to take back this land from the Muslims, and he needs our help. Take a few days to decide what you want to do."

This sounds very important. You would be fighting a crusade to protect the whole Christian world.

If you are killed in the Holy Land, Pope Urban has promised to issue a document called an indulgence. It will forgive your sins in this life.

But not everyone can go. The lord will need knights to stay behind and protect the village.

➵ *To stay behind, turn to page* **22**.

➵ *To fight in the Crusade, turn to page* **23**.

Lord Humbert and several knights decide to make the long journey to Jerusalem. It will take them at least a year.

You stay behind to watch over the village. One night, you wake up. "Help!" you hear the villagers screaming. You rush outside.

Armed men are attacking your village. You realize they are outlaws who live in the woods and attack travelers. Now they are attacking villages because so many men are gone.

You grab your dagger and sword and rush to fight the outlaws. Servants and villagers join you, but the outlaws outnumber you. You could ride to another village to get help. But can you get back in time?

→ *To stay and fight, turn to page* **35**.

→ *To ride for help, turn to page* **36**.

Both knights and foot soldiers left France to fight in the First Crusade.

You decide to join the crusade to the Holy Land. In August 1096, you start a journey that will cover about 2,000 miles. You travel by horseback through the south of France into Italy. You cross the Adriatic Sea by boat. You then ride through the Byzantine Empire to its capital, Constantinople.

Turn the page.

When you reach Constantinople in April 1097, you're amazed at the size of the army. More than 30,000 people have come together to fight the Muslims. There aren't many knights in the group. Most of the soldiers are peasants, monks, and priests.

Over the next two years, the army battles its way through Asia Minor and Syria. In June 1099, the force finally reaches Jerusalem. Your army has lost more than half of its soldiers to battle, disease, and starvation. Luckily, you've managed to stay alive.

The Muslims, known as Saracens, have strongly defended the city. Walls up to 50 feet high and 10 feet thick surround the city. Your army will have to take Jerusalem by siege. You'll need to keep the Saracens from running away.

During the next three weeks, you and the other soldiers build weapons and equipment for the siege. You fight your thirst in the blazing sun as you build ladders, trebuchets, and a battering ram. You also build two siege towers that are more than 50 feet tall. The height of the towers will allow soldiers to climb over Jerusalem's high walls.

By July 14, your force splits into two. One group will attack the city's northern wall. The other will attack from the south. You must decide where you're going to fight.

➵ To attack from the north, turn to page **26**.

➵ To attack from the south, turn to page **34**.

Your force attacks at dawn. You load missiles into the trebuchets and fire them at the city's outer walls. Under the cover of the missiles, another group of soldiers moves the huge battering ram to the walls. The soldiers crash the ram through the outer walls into the main city walls.

The Saracens pour flaming tar and wax down on the ram, setting it on fire. Your soldiers put out the fire, but then realize that they can't pull the ram away from the walls. With the ram blocking the hole, there's no way the siege tower can reach the inner walls.

You leave your post at the trebuchet and run over to the men struggling with the ram. "Set it on fire!" you shout. "It's the only way!" The other men look at you like you're crazy, but they obey.

Battering rams were used to invade castles and cities throughout the Middle Ages.

As the battering ram burns to ashes, the men cheer. They now have a clear entry into the inner walls of the city.

During the second day of the siege, you join a group moving the three-story siege tower toward the inner walls. The tower is filled with soldiers and rests on wheels. If you can get the tower to a wall, soldiers will climb into the city. Inside, they will fight hand-to-hand with the Saracens.

Turn the page.

Soldiers used a siege tower to scale Jerusalem's walls and enter the city.

But it's not easy to move the tower. Sweat pours off your face as you and dozens of other soldiers inch forward. You duck as the Saracens fire blazing arrows and hurl stones at the tower.

Finally, the tower reaches a wall. Those in the top of the tower fire arrows and throw stones back at the Saracens. Thick smoke pours out of the city. Behind the smoke cover, soldiers leap over the wall. You quickly climb to the top of the tower and follow them.

Amid your screams and shouts, the Saracens flee. Some attempt to escape by jumping from the walls. Before long, the crusaders take over the city. More than 10,000 Saracens die at the hands of the Christian soldiers. To your horror, some soldiers even kill women and children. But when it's over, Jerusalem is under Christian control.

You now face a decision. You could return home. It would be another long journey, but you would be well rewarded by your lord for your service. But many knights are staying in the Holy Land. You've contained the Saracens, but they are likely to rise up again.

➤ *To return home, turn to page* **38**.

➤ *To stay in the Holy Land, turn to page* **39**.

The knights gather at the stables and get their horses ready. You know there's an extra horse that you can use. You slip into the horse's stall without anyone noticing.

You put on a leather tunic and leather trousers. Over that, you pull on a shirt made of metal links called mail. The mail shirt will help protect your chest. Your iron helmet fits over your head. The helmet is heavy and makes breathing difficult. But at least no one will recognize you.

When you get to the neighboring village, the fight is well under way. You spot an enemy knight by himself at the edge of the battle. You speed toward him, your sword high in the air. You take aim, hoping your sword strikes a spot where the links in the mail shirt weren't fastened properly. It does. The other knight falls to the ground. You feel a rush of victory.

But then, you feel a sharp stab high in your back, near your arm. You turn to see another enemy knight pull a dagger from your back. You become dizzy and fall from your horse. As a pool of blood forms on the ground beneath you, everything fades to black. You die before you even get a chance to become a knight.

THE END

To follow another path, turn to page 11.
To read the conclusion, turn to page 101.

During the early Middle Ages, knights wore clothing made of mail.

Jeffrey is huge. He rides a large, sturdy fighting horse called a destrier. His armor appears strong. His lance is large and new, and its metal tip is shiny. It's much nicer than the dented one you use.

The fight begins. Jeffrey is quick, and he strikes often at you. At one point, he slashes your cheek. You hold your hand to your face and look at him with surprise. You didn't expect the melee to be this rough.

Jeffrey continues the attack, and he quickly gets you to the ground. You're disappointed, as this means you'll have to give him your horse and equipment. What will you do without them?

As you hurry to stand up, you feel a sharp pain in your side. You look down and realize that you've run right into Jeffrey's lance. Its sharp point pierced a weak spot in your mail shirt. Jeffrey looks startled. "I didn't mean to stab you!" he cries.

Your fellow knights rush to your side, but it's too late. There's nothing they can do to stop the bleeding. You die there on the ground.

33

THE END

To follow another path, turn to page 11.
To read the conclusion, turn to page 101.

On the south side of Jerusalem, fighting is fierce. The Saracens expected the attack to come from this side, and now you face their strongest troops. Flaming arrows and large rocks fly all around you. You move toward the wall. Just then, a large mallet flies past your head. You duck and turn around just in time to see it strike a fellow knight. It kills him instantly.

The fighting starts to wind down as the sun sets. You hope tomorrow will be more successful.

You walk slowly toward the crusaders' camp outside the city. But suddenly, you feel a sharp blow to the back of your head. The Saracens weren't finished attacking after all. You fall to your knees. You become one of the thousands who die in the battle for Jerusalem.

THE END

To follow another path, turn to page 11.
To read the conclusion, turn to page 101.

There's no time to run for help. You'll have to protect your village on your own.

You see a group of outlaws running out of your house. Their arms are full of food and supplies. One of your servants leaps on a man whose arms are full of linens. The outlaw reaches up and stabs your servant in the shoulder. You raise your sword and run screaming toward the outlaw. Your sword finds its target, and the outlaw drops dead.

Suddenly, you feel a sharp pain in your back. Another outlaw has stabbed you. As blood pours from your wound, you sink to your knees. All of your knightly training cannot stop you from dying at the hands of the outlaws.

THE END

To follow another path, turn to page 11.
To read the conclusion, turn to page 101.

Some knights rode large, powerful horses called destriers.

You race to the stables and hurl yourself onto your horse. You raise the whip, urging the horse to gallop faster and faster. Once you reach the nearest village, you leap to the ground and run to the house of the village knight.

"Let me in!" you shout as you pound on the door. "I've come from the next village, and we're under attack by outlaws!"

The knight is gone to the Holy Land. But several of his squires and servants mount horses and rush with you back to your village. As you ride, you pray that you aren't too late.

When you reach your village, the outlaws are still there. Several dead villagers lie in the street. With the help of the neighboring men, you're able to kill or capture all of the outlaws. You've done your duty as a knight. You look forward to defending your village for years to come.

37

THE END

To follow another path, turn to page 11.
To read the conclusion, turn to page 101.

You've had enough of fighting in a strange land. The memories of the killing of innocent people still haunt you. You start out for your village. Because you aren't fighting battles along the way, the trip takes only about a year this time.

Lord Humbert has also returned safely. He speaks to you one day.

"You have served courageously," he says. "Some knights, as you know, have not returned. Two villages need your leadership. The crops there grow well. I know you will have success."

"Thank you, my lord," you say. It's an honor for a knight to be put in charge of two villages.

Every year you grow wealthier. Your villagers respect you. You look back on your life with much pride.

THE END

To follow another path, turn to page 11.
To read the conclusion, turn to page 101.

You decide to stay for a time in Jerusalem. One day, you meet a man named Gerard who runs a Christian hospital in Jerusalem.

"I need men who can protect this hospital from the Saracens," Gerard tells you. "We have won Jerusalem, but they still remain a threat. Will you join me?"

You agree. You work with Gerard until he retires as head of the hospital in 1118. Two years later, Gerard's successor, Raymond du Puy, makes the Hospitaliers of St. John a military group of knights. You take the vows of a monk and become one of the Knights of Justice. You live the rest of your life in Jerusalem as a member of the Hospitaliers. You're proud you helped create one of the most successful knightly organizations.

THE END

To follow another path, turn to page 11.
To read the conclusion, turn to page 101.

Every squire hoped to someday become a knight.

CHAPTER 3

The Quest to Conquer France

It's a sunny summer day in 1346. You're grooming your horse in the stable when your lord's messenger hurries through the doorway.

"Lord John wants to see you and all of the squires right away," he says. He walks away as quickly as he came.

You put away the grooming brush and head toward the manor house. What might the lord want? Maybe he'll tell you that you're ready to become a knight. After all, you're 18. You've been training for knighthood most of your life. You can expertly use a lance and dagger. You can defend yourself with a shield, and you treat people with respect and courtesy.

Turn the page.

At the large stone house, all the squires are excited and a bit nervous. Lord John sits at a table. He motions for everyone to quiet down.

"As you all know, England is at war with France." You nod your head. The French began attacking English territories and ports in 1337. Since then, King Edward III has sent English troops to fight in France.

The lord continues. "The lords in this region have now been asked to join the fight." All the squires break out in chatter. "Quiet!" Lord John orders. "I will need some of you to go into battle with me. Others need to stay behind and look after this manor and my other villages while I'm away. We need to be on guard against attacks by the Scots from the north." You are familiar with the fight against the Scottish. They have long wanted to be independent from England.

"For those who stay behind, I will make you knights right away. If you join me in battle, knighthood will have to wait until you prove your bravery on the battlefield." Lord John pauses. "You must make your decision today. Tomorrow, we prepare to leave for France."

What should you do? As a knight, you will be given a village to oversee. But some knights who come back from France are very rich. After expenses are paid and the nobles take their share, the knights divide the remaining captured treasures. Of course, some men who go to France never return.

➻ To stay behind, turn to page 44.

➻ To go to France, turn to page 45.

Before Lord John leaves, he knights you and others who will stay behind. Before the ceremony, you and the other squires dress all in white. The lord taps each of you on the shoulder with his sword. He buckles a new sword and lance on your belt. You don't receive a full suit of armor yet, as they are very expensive.

Knighthood makes you a good candidate for marriage. Before he left, Lord John suggested that you court his niece, Anne. She comes from a wealthy, powerful family. You would inherit much land and money if you married her.

But for several months, you've been secretly courting Sarah, a young woman from the village. Her father is a serf. Sarah is not rich, but you love her. Should you go against Lord John?

➤ *To marry Anne, turn to page **48**.*

➤ *To marry Sarah, turn to page **49**.*

Six weeks ago, you arrived in France and met up with other English troops. As part of a large army, you marched east, battling in towns such as Caen, Brionne, and Poissy. Hundreds of your men died along the way, either from sickness or injuries. Now you find yourself at a small village called Crécy.

It's the evening of August 25. The day before, your army of about 12,000 soldiers crossed the River Somme on its way north. Soon after you crossed, the French army appeared on the river's south bank. It looked as if there might be a battle. But King Philip IV of France turned his army around and headed east.

A fellow soldier turns to you at the campfire. "Did you see the size of the French army? They must have three times the soldiers we do. To fight them is sure death."

Turn the page.

English knights and soldiers rested before the Battle of Crécy.

"I trust King Edward," you say. "He would rather back out than risk an embarrassing defeat." You try to sound confident, but you are worried.

The next day, King Edward guides the army to the top of a slope. He divides the soldiers into three groups to fight in the front, middle, and rear of the battle.

The king takes position in a windmill at the top of the slope. From there, he can see all of the battle. Thick woods are behind you. The French can approach you only through a wide valley.

"Quickly," a fellow squire says to you. "We are needed on the front lines to fight with Edward, the young prince." You nod. Edward of Woodstock is the king's son. He's only 16, but he is brave and smart. You start to head to the front. Just then, someone tugs at your arm.

"You there, young lad." It's a messenger. "We need more people in the rear guard to help defend against surprise attack. Will you help us?"

➤ To protect the rear guard, turn to page 52.

➤ To fight up front, turn to page 55.

On a beautiful Sunday, you marry Anne in her family's castle. Your wife is kind and pleasant. You think it will be a good match, even if you don't love her deeply.

Several weeks pass. Lord John and many of the manor's knights and squires are still in France. Messengers tell you that Scots are approaching your village. You must put together a small force to defend the village. But because of the war in France, few knights remain. You gather some squires and even order serfs to help.

One day you hear yelling and shouting near the outskirts of the village. The Scots are here! You have better weapons, but they have more men. Should you try to travel to other villages and find more men to fight?

➤ *To round up more troops, turn to page* **63**.

➤ *To stay and fight, turn to page* **64**.

Anne is not happy with your decision to marry Sarah. She is sure to tell Lord John when he returns. But you're happy to be married to the most beautiful, kind girl in the world.

Three weeks after the wedding, you and Sarah travel to the big annual market in the next village. You bring a bag of money. You plan to buy a sword at the village blacksmith shop.

Before the market opens, you attend services at the village's large church. Hundreds of people are there. Everyone for miles around has come to the market.

After the service, Sarah walks among the stalls set up in the town square. You stop at the blacksmith shop and find a sword you like. You reach for the money bag that you have tied around your waist. It's not there.

"Someone took my money!" you gasp.

People came from miles around to village markets, like this one at Westminster.

"It must have happened in the church," Sarah says. The market attracts not only buyers and sellers, but also thieves. Someone has expertly cut your bag from your belt.

At home, you think about what to do. There's an opportunity for quick riches if you go to war in France. But you could be killed. Maybe you should stay home and try to earn back the money.

→ To go to France, go to page **51**.

→ To stay in England, turn to page **57**.

"I must go to France," you tell Sarah. "There I will have a chance to capture treasure."

You travel to the south of England by horseback. At the coast, you meet up with other soldiers heading to France. You travel by ship across the English Channel.

In France, you hear news of the English army. King Edward, his son Prince Edward, and their troops have marched through several towns, defeating the French along the way. They are traveling east toward a village called Crécy. You follow the others who are heading that way.

Turn to page 55.

The French outnumbered the English at the Battle of Crécy.

It's late in the afternoon of August 26 as you take your position in the rear guard. Behind you is a circle of wagons and carts that protect the army's baggage and horses.

Shouts come from the front of the battlefield. You see only a blur of bodies, horses, and arrows. The French have started the attack. If the front lines don't hold them back, they will be marching closer toward you.

Suddenly, you catch a quick movement out of the corner of your eye. A dozen or so French knights are closing in on the wagon circle. "At the back! French!" you shout. Several soldiers in the rear guard swing around to fight. This attack on both the front and rear lines could be a huge blow to your army.

A few soldiers on both sides are on horseback, but you and most of the other troops are on foot. You handle your sword expertly, thanks to your years of training. Fierce fighting continues for several minutes. Swords and lances clash and clang. Men scream and yell as sharp weapons pierce their skin. Your force manages to overpower the French soldiers. Those not killed or injured run away.

Two French knights lie bleeding on the ground. By the looks of their armor, they are rich.

Turn the page.

"These men will bring a good ransom if we take them as hostages," one of your fellow soldiers says.

"But the king doesn't want us to take hostages," someone else says. "He says dealing with hostages distracts us from our goal of victory for the entire English army."

➤ To let the hostages go, turn to page **59**.
➤ To hold the hostages for ransom, turn to page **61**.

You ride to the front lines. The attack has already started. Deadly metal bolts are soaring toward you, released by the French army's crossbows. But your army's archers use longbows. These weapons shoot many arrows in the time that it takes a crossbow to shoot one bolt.

But your archers can't stop every French soldier. The enemy knights surround young Prince Edward. They attack him with swords and lances. The prince is forced off his horse, and he falls to his knees. On the ground, he is in even more danger.

The Earl of Warwick turns to you and another knight. "Run back to the king and tell him his son is in danger! We need more knights up here!"

Turn the page.

Young Prince Edward (right) defended himself against French soldiers.

You don't want to waste time running to the king. The prince needs your help now.

To find the king, turn to page **66**.

To help the prince, turn to page **70**.

Several months pass. Sarah is grateful that you've stayed home. But times are hard. There's been a drought. The lack of rain hurts the crops. When crops don't grow, serfs can't give you and the lord your share.

One day, while working in the fields, you hear the galloping of horses. You look up to see Lord John and your fellow knights, back from war. The knights are wearing new coats of armor and hold shiny swords. You can see fat pouches hanging from the sides of the horses. No doubt they are filled with jewels and gold coins.

Lord John rides over and gets off his horse. "I've spoken with my niece," he says. "I heard that you chose not to marry her." He shakes his head. "From the looks of things around here, that was not a wise decision." You want to defend yourself, but keep silent.

Turn the page.

Lord John continues. "I need someone I can trust in charge of this village. You purposely went against my wishes. I have no choice but to give control of the village to another knight."

You knew it might come to this, but you still are ashamed. The bright future you imagined for yourself is gone. Now you'll have to leave your home and find another way to support yourself and Sarah. You married the woman you loved, but you ended up losing everything else.

THE END

To follow another path, turn to page 11.
To read the conclusion, turn to page 101.

English soldiers' longbows helped them gain the upper hand during the battle.

"We should follow the king's orders," you say. "Let the French knights go."

At this point, the front lines of your army are fighting off the French attack. You are amazed because the French outnumber you. But the English army's position on the slope gives it an advantage. Also, your archers are using longbows. The French soldiers are using crossbows, which take a long time to reload. Your archers can shoot many arrows before the French release one metal bolt from a crossbow.

Turn the page.

By midnight, the bodies of more than 1,000 French soldiers cover the battlefield. King Philip has retreated, and your army has won.

Early the next morning, King Edward comes to your division to congratulate everyone. Someone tells him about the hostages and the decision to let them go.

"Very good," says the king. "I don't want to deal with hostages. The only thing I want is more victories such as this one."

He turns to you and the others. "Thank you for respecting my wishes. For this, I will make you knights today. You will receive a village as soon as we return home."

Your heart leaps. You will soon be a knight.

THE END

To follow another path, turn to page 11.
To read the conclusion, turn to page 101.

The prospect of gaining riches is too tempting. "Let's keep them as hostages," you tell the others.

By midnight, the battle is over. You thought that the French would win because of their army's size. But the French crossbowmen and knights proved to be no match for your soldiers and archers.

The king rides on horseback to your division. He sees the wounded French knights, who are now sitting up.

"What are these men doing here?" King Edward demands.

"They are hostages, your highness," you say respectfully. "Surely we'll be able to gain a large sum for them."

Turn the page.

The king glares at you. "Did you not hear what I said earlier? I said I do not want any hostages! We can't be sidetracked with making deals with the French. Let them go!"

He looks at you and the other soldiers. "By disrespecting my wishes, you have put into danger your chance of becoming knights. I need people I can trust." He rides away as you quickly untie the hostages.

Your army has won the Battle of Crécy, but you may have ruined your chances at knighthood.

THE END

To follow another path, turn to page 11.
To read the conclusion, turn to page 101.

"Please don't go," Anne begs. "What about us here in the village? What about me?"

"I will take you to the bailiff's house," you reply. "You'll be safe under his care."

It takes a couple of days, but you return with many men. You hope the villagers were able to hold off the attack. Miles away, you see smoke in the sky. As you get closer to the village, houses are burning. You see no one. Your heart sinks.

You ride first to the bailiff's house. "Hello?" you shout. But there's no answer. Inside, you find the bodies of Anne, the bailiff, and his wife. You've lost everything — your crops, your home, and your wife. You wonder how you will rebuild your life after such a heartbreaking event.

THE END

To follow another path, turn to page 11.
To read the conclusion, turn to page 101.

During raids, attackers stole everything they could carry away with them.

The Scots are tough. You can't leave now. You hope you and the others will be able to defend the village.

The Scots use archers to launch an attack on the village. All of your experienced archers are in France. Your armor helps to protect you from the arrows. But few of your villagers have armor or swords. Their only weapons are heavy shovels and maces. The Scots' arrows have killed many of the villagers.

You hear Anne scream. You turn back and find that some Scots have entered the manor house. You lunge at a man who is holding Anne. Your sword pierces his chest, and he lets her go.

"Run!" you tell Anne. She escapes. But several men surround you, swords raised. The blades reach their targets, and you collapse on the floor. As you take your last breath, you're grateful that at least you died defending your home and family.

THE END

To follow another path, turn to page 11.
To read the conclusion, turn to page 101.

Sir Thomas Norwich (center) asked King Edward to send help for the prince.

You find King Edward at the back of the army, near the windmill.

"Your highness," you say. "Your son is under attack from the French. His life is in danger. I respectfully request assistance from your division."

The king looks at you. "I will do no such thing. The boy must learn to fight on his own. Let him win his spurs."

You race back to the front. The fighting is fierce, and you can't get near the prince. For several hours, you fight the French in hand-to-hand combat. You hope the prince will survive.

Every time you turn around, another French soldier swings his sword at you. You grow tired from ducking the blows in the growing darkness. A few times, swords noisily clang against your armor, but it protects you.

You manage to disarm many French soldiers with your lance and sword. Other English knights do the same. Hundreds of French knights lie dead on the battlefield. Around midnight, King Philip and his knights retreat. Your army has won, but you stay in fighting position for the rest of the night.

Turn the page.

As the sun rises that morning, you see the prince sitting on the battlefield, surrounded by knights. He appears to be safe. Soon, the king appears and talks to his son.

"These men saved my life," the prince tells his father. "They should be rewarded greatly for their service to the crown."

The king agrees. "Tomorrow I will knight the squires who helped protect my son. Those of you who are knights will receive another reward."

Your heart sinks. You were not with the prince in battle. You will not receive any reward from the king. You only hope that you will survive the battles with the French that are sure to come.

THE END

To follow another path, turn to page 11.
To read the conclusion, turn to page 101.

Prince Edward knelt before his father after fighting bravely during the battle.

You decide to help the prince. The other knight rides away to seek help from the king.

You dig in your spurs and race toward the prince. Just then, a French knight thrusts his sword at you. You nearly lose your balance but manage to stay upright. You strike a blow at the French knight, and he falls to the ground. But other French knights continue the attack.

The battle is furious, yet no help arrives. You wonder why the king has not sent more troops to the front. You know he must have a good reason.

By midnight, hundreds of French knights lie dead at your feet. The ones still alive have retreated. As soon as the danger passes, the prince sits down to rest. He has a few cuts but isn't seriously hurt.

Early the next morning, the king arrives. He and the prince have a long talk. Afterward, the king rides over to you and the other men.

"My son tells me of your bravery" he says. "To show my appreciation, I will knight those of you who are squires. Those who are knights will receive another reward when we return to England."

Your heart leaps at the king's praise. You're glad you made the right decision.

THE END

To follow another path, turn to page 11.
To read the conclusion, turn to page 101.

In 1517, Martin Luther nailed a list of complaints about the Catholic Church to the door of Castle Church.

CHAPTER 4

Revolt of the Peasants

It's late in the winter of 1525. You and other knights gather in the town hall for an important meeting. Conflict threatens to divide your village and Germany as a whole.

During the past several years, you've fought in many battles. It seems that everyone is involved in the fighting — noble lords, political leaders, even priests. Arguments about taxes and highway tolls end in bloody fights.

The latest disagreement centers on religion. A former monk, Martin Luther, is leading a reform of the Catholic Church.

Turn the page.

Luther believes that the church has become corrupt. He's especially upset that some churches are selling indulgences, which are documents that promise forgiveness of a person's sins. Luther's followers are called Protestants. Although Luther doesn't support violence against the church, some of his followers do.

Peasants all over Germany are angry with the ruling class, which is mainly Catholic. By law, peasants must pay taxes and give a share of their crops to their lord. Lords often make unfair laws and demands. Peasants need permission from the lord to get married and even to hunt and fish. When a peasant dies, the lord can take everything he owns. Nothing is left for his family.

Many peasants have decided to revolt against the church in the hope of improving their lives. Tonight the villagers must decide whether to remain with the Catholics or join the Protestants.

By the end of the evening, the villagers decide to join other peasants in the revolt. Some knights are joining the peasants in the fight. They are becoming rich as peasants attack churches and abbeys and seize their treasures. But if you remain with the Catholic ruling class, you could rise up the ranks. One day you could become a wealthy lord.

→ To remain with the Catholics, turn to page 76.

→ To join the peasant revolt, turn to page 78.

Charles V ruled the Holy Roman Empire from 1519 to 1556.

You decide not to join the peasants. There are many of them, but you don't think they can beat the powerful church.

You join the Swabian League, an army that protects towns and villages in southwestern Germany. The league is loyal to the nobles, priests, and Emperor Charles V of the Holy Roman Empire. The empire includes Germany and many other countries in Central Europe.

The Swabian League wants to put down the peasant revolt. But it won't be easy. Many experienced knights are fighting wars elsewhere in Europe. At the same time, the peasant force is growing each day.

You can try to round up as many men as you can find and fight the peasants now. Or you can try to make a deal with the peasants. That delay would give you time to find more knights.

→ *To gather troops, turn to page 80.*

→ *To deal with the peasants, turn to page 81.*

You've long been troubled by the corruption in the Catholic Church. The peasants need strong leadership for their revolution to succeed. You agree to lead them. You hope that the peasants will receive their rights without violence.

For a while, the peasants wait for their demands to be settled. Then they become impatient. They decide to march to the next town, where the lord and church leaders live. You're not sure this is a good idea, but you go with them anyway.

When you get there, the peasants approach the town's abbey, where the priests and monks live. "You are surrounded!" the peasants shout. "Give us your money and treasures, or we will destroy the abbey and all of you with it!"

A monk comes out of the abbey. "Please don't hurt us," he begs. "We will pay you 5,000 gulden to leave us alone."

The rebels were upset that priests and monks were selling indulgences.

"No!" the peasants shout. "That amount isn't enough to make up for how we've been treated! We want everything!" The peasants move forward, waving their weapons angrily.

You want the peasants' demands to be taken seriously. But these holy men are unarmed. You think it would be an unfair fight.

➻ To raid the abbey and village, turn to page 83.

➻ To make a deal, turn to page 85.

You ride to the nearby villages. Perhaps there are some squires who would be willing to fight. Or maybe some knights who have been fighting in foreign countries have returned. You might even be able to convince peasants to fight for the Swabian League instead of joining the rebellion.

You find some young men willing to fight. But the more experienced knights have not yet returned. You also discover that most of the peasants have left to join the peasant rebellion.

When you return with your new troops, the fight against the peasants is in full swing.

80

Turn to page 94.

The peasant leaders agree to meet with you and other Swabian League knights. They bring a list of their demands called the Twelve Articles. While the talks take place, you send several knights to neighboring villages to gather any soldiers they can find.

The negotiations take several days. When they are over, the peasants have more rights. They are free to fish and hunt for themselves. They can carry weapons. And they won't be punished if they marry without the lord's permission.

When the meeting is over, you learn more troops have arrived. You send word about the soldiers to the Swabian League council in the city of Ulm. They've been preparing for an attack against the peasants all along. After a few days, a messenger brings news that the council has declared war upon the peasants.

Turn the page.

"But I thought we had a deal with you!" one of the peasant leaders says.

"We can't just let you walk away," you tell him. "You still pose a threat to us and to the emperor."

The angry peasants leave and immediately begin an attack on the town. But as the fighting starts, you realize you still have fewer troops than the peasants do.

➤ To stay and fight, turn to page **94**.

➤ To find more troops, turn to page **95**.

On April 16, 1525, the peasant army attacked the town of Weinsburg.

The peasants waste no time bursting into the homes of nobles. You hear screams and shouts mixed with the thuds of someone being hit with a musket or shovel.

You enter the abbey. Over the centuries, many believers have given money and treasures to the church. Inside you find rich treasures, such as statues, jewels, and gold and silver crosses. Even the vestments the priests wear are made of the most expensive cloth.

Turn the page.

As you touch a soft robe, Jakob Wehe bursts into the room. He is a priest who supports the peasants and has become one of their leaders.

"The Swabian League is outside the town walls! They are ready to attack!" he says breathlessly. "If they find us, they will kill us. I'm going to escape. I suggest you do the same if you want to spare your life."

If you escape, you'll be abandoning your troops. But Jakob is right. The Swabian League soldiers are loyal to the church and the nobles. If they find you, they will kill you.

➤ *To stay, turn to page* **86**.

➤ *To try to escape, turn to page* **92**.

You and the peasant leaders enter the building. You speak with the priests and monks.

"We won't harm you if you let us take your belongings," you tell them. "We want your furniture, books, gold, silver, and jewels. We will take you hostage and hold you for ransom, but we won't hurt you." The priests nod. They have no way to stop you.

"The peasants are well armed and greatly outnumber you," you continue. "Allow us to overtake the town, and we won't harm anyone."

A messenger sends word to the nobles that you want a ransom for the holy men. They pay you well. Not only have you collected treasures, but now you also have a nice sum of money. You decide that raiding towns and churches isn't such a bad thing after all.

Turn to page **89**.

"I won't abandon my troops," you tell Jakob. "Leave if you must. I will stay here."

Jakob pauses for a moment and then runs from the room.

You hear clanging and clashing of swords, mixed with the sound of gunfire. Shouts and screams follow. You dash outside to help in the fighting.

You expertly wield your sword and manage to kill or wound several solders. Just then, you spot a large Swabian League knight running into some nearby woods. You decide to chase after him. But your armor weighs you down. Gasping for breath, you stop to rest. When you turn around, two Swabian knights stand in front of you. Each grabs one of your arms.

"You! Are you the leader of this gang?" one knight asks you.

"Yes, I am," you reply.

"You will die for your part in this rebellion."

Your heart skips a beat. You thought it might come to this. But you realize you are not ready to die. There must be a way out.

"Before you kill me, grant me one last request," you tell the knights. "Let me speak to your commander."

"Why should we?" one of them sneers at you.

"I have taken the vows of knighthood, just as you have," you plead. "Please do this for a brother knight."

Grudgingly, the knights agree.

87

Turn to page 96.

Well-armed Swabian League knights fought the peasant rebels.

For many days, you march through the countryside. Peasants in other villages join you. Soon you have several thousand troops.

You arrive at a large town with an abbey and many fine houses. You camp outside the walls and decide to wait until the morning to raid.

As the sun rises, you and your soldiers scale the town's walls. The streets are empty, and you think this will be an easy raid. But suddenly, well-armed knights appear, swords drawn.

"It's the Swabian League!" a peasant shouts.

The Swabian League is your main enemy. For many years, the Swabian League has protected the cities of southwestern Germany. They support the priests, the nobles, and the emperor. They will not go down without a fight.

Turn the page.

The battle is lopsided from the start. The peasants wear only their clothes, while the Swabian League knights wear heavy armor. The peasants are on foot, and the knights have horses. Some of the peasants have muskets, but most are armed only with shovels and mallets. The knights have swords and lances. They easily dodge the peasants' clumsy blows. Their weapons pierce the peasants' thin trousers and shirts. Men, women, and even children lie dying on the ground.

If you continue fighting, your losses may be huge. You're near the Swabian League headquarters. Maybe you can speak to the commander and make a deal.

➤ *To suggest a retreat, go to page **91**.*
➤ *To try to make a deal, turn to page **96**.*

"Maybe we should back down," you suggest to the peasant leader.

"Are you crazy?" he shouts. "We cannot quit now. What kind of leader are you? If you desert us, we will kill you!"

The fighting gets heavier. All around you, knights of the Swabian League are killing peasants. There is no way that you can win this battle.

You joined this fight because you thought the peasants could win and bring about reform in the Catholic Church. Now that looks impossible. Even if you survive this battle, you will be viewed as the enemy. Should you continue fighting? Or try to save your own life?

➤ *To try to save your life, turn to page 97.*

➤ *To keep fighting, turn to page 98.*

In May 1525, the Swabian league defeated the peasants at Frankenhausen.

Jakob knows about secret tunnels that lead to the Danube River. You are able to get to the river unnoticed. Once there, you hide in a cave.

After several hours, you hear dogs barking. The Swabian League soldiers are hunting for you. As the barks get closer, your heart races. You look at Jakob with fear in your eyes. Soon, the dogs are barking nonstop at the front of the cave. Two men burst in with guns and grab you and Jakob from your hiding place.

The men bind your arms and legs and take you to a grassy meadow. Six other captured men are there as well. You see a large block of wood.

"Any last words?" a soldier asks as he leads you and Jakob to the block. A large, gleaming ax lies nearby.

Jakob is murmuring a prayer as you lay your head down on the block. It's the last thing you ever hear.

THE END

To follow another path, turn to page 11.
To read the conclusion, turn to page 101.

The strength of the peasants surprises you. They have muskets and daggers. Some also carry shovels and other heavy tools.

Your army is outnumbered. You kill some peasants, but every time you turn around, another one attacks you. You duck and swerve, trying to dodge shots and sword blows. Around you, knights are falling to the ground.

As you're attacking one peasant, you feel a sharp blow to your ribs. The pain is piercing. You turn around and face your attacker. He smiles. You start to feel faint, and you fall to the ground. The dirt around you is stained red with your blood. Your life ends at the hands of a peasant.

THE END

To follow another path, turn to page 11.
To read the conclusion, turn to page 101.

You ride to neighboring towns. You convince every young man to fight with you. They are very young, just 13 or 14, but you are desperate.

You ride back to the town with your new soldiers. As the battle continues, your army is losing troops. The peasants might win.

The young men of your army may not be strong, but they are quick. They escape musket blasts and dagger blows. They deliver piercing blows with their own daggers.

Soon the course of the battle takes a turn. After several hours, your soldiers win. In the coming weeks, peasants throughout the region meet a similar fate. When it's over, at least 100,000 peasants are dead. The Peasants' War becomes one of the deadliest wars ever fought on German soil.

THE END

To follow another path, turn to page 11.
To read the conclusion, turn to page 101.

You're at the Swabian League headquarters. "We can't win," you tell the league commander. "I'm willing to order my troops to retreat."

"And what about you? What should we do with such a traitor?" the commander asks.

"I was forced by the rebels to lead them," you lie. "Please grant me mercy. I had no choice. They would have killed me if I hadn't joined them."

"You appear to be a wealthy man," the commander says. "You are worth a large ransom, I'm sure. We will hold you until someone pays for your release."

The Swabian League soldiers win the battle, and you're a hostage. But at least you're still alive.

THE END

To follow another path, turn to page 11.
To read the conclusion, turn to page 101.

You sneak away during the fighting. You find a Swabian League officer and ask to see the commander.

"I want to fight for you," you tell the commander. "I am willing to abandon my troops. It is clear that we're going to lose. I've collected many treasures during these battles. I will give you everything I have."

The commander agrees. You switch sides and pledge loyalty to the emperor. You stand back and watch as the peasants continue to die in large numbers. Several weeks later, the rebellion is put down. At least 100,000 peasants die. You're glad to be alive but know that you have shamed yourself as a knight. You will live with that knowledge for the rest of your life.

THE END

To follow another path, turn to page 11.
To read the conclusion, turn to page 101.

About 100,000 peasants died during the war.

You think back to your knightly training. One of the things you learned was the importance of chivalry. Part of that code means keeping your word. It's clear that the peasants are going to lose. But you promised them that you would lead them, even when fighting becomes difficult.

You attack the enemy with renewed energy. Maybe there is a way out of this after all. You kill several Swabian League knights. You plunge your sword into the gaps of their armor. Suddenly you feel a sharp pain under your arm.

You whirl around and see a Swabian League knight on his horse. His lance sticks out of your body. You fall to the ground, gasping for breath.

You thought it might end this way. But you have kept your word. You die as you lived — an honorable knight.

THE END

To follow another path, turn to page 11.
To read the conclusion, turn to page 101.

The Third Crusade to the
Holy Land took place between
1189 and 1192.

CHAPTER 5

The End of an Era

Knights played an important part in the Crusades. There were nine of these battles for control of the Middle East between 1096 and the late 1200s. Overall, the Crusades were unsuccessful. Muslims kept control of Jerusalem and the surrounding area.

Knights also were important in the Hundred Years' War (1337–1453) between England and France. In 1453, France won the war and reclaimed most of the territory that England captured during earlier battles.

Knighthood started to decline in the 1500s. By that time, craftsmen had discovered a better way to make gunpowder. Cannons and guns, which could be fired from long distances, replaced swords and daggers on the battlefield. The accuracy of longbows and crossbows improved, which also allowed fighting from a distance. Armies no longer relied as much on hand-to-hand combat.

Kings raised large standing armies of soldiers, which were easier to maintain and train than armies of knights. Instead of fighting, knights oversaw villages and farmers. The title of knight became a symbolic honor.

But you can still find references to knights today. The Knights of Columbus is a Catholic service organization formed in 1882. Its founding members pledged to defend their faith, their country, and their families.

Some knightly organizations are thought to be secretive. The Knights Templar was founded around 1119 to protect Christian pilgrims visiting Jerusalem. They became powerful and rich, and leaders such as kings and popes wanted to stop them. Many Templars were burned at the stake in 1307. In 1312, Pope Clement V dissolved the group. But mysteries and stories about them continue, such as in the best-selling book *The Da Vinci Code* by Dan Brown.

Today in England, you will find symbolic knighting ceremonies. The king or queen grants honorary knighthood to people who have made important contributions to society and culture. Recent knightings include singers Elton John and Paul McCartney and actors Sean Connery and Ian McKellen. Men receive the title "Sir." Women, such as actress Judi Dench, are called "Dame."

The Knights Templar's original mission was to protect Christians in the Holy Land.

More than 500 years after the last knights fought in battle, they continue to capture our imaginations. People at Renaissance fairs around the country reenact the time of the knights. At a Renaissance festival, you can watch jousting tournaments and buy swords and armor.

Knights are even found in science fiction. The popular *Star Wars* movies feature Jedi Knights who fight to protect the universe.

In the Middle Ages, people admired knights for their bravery, courage, and position in society. They were seen as defenders of countries and people. Even though knights no longer fight battles and joust in tournaments, the ideals they stood for still live on.

TIME LINE

1096–1099 — The First Crusade takes place.

1113 — Pope Paschal II recognizes the Friars of the Hospital of St. John of Jerusalem, which later becomes known as the Hospitaliers of St. John.

1147–1149 — Louis VII of France and Conrad III of Germany lead the Second Crusade.

1189–1192 — Philip II of France, Frederick I of Germany, and Richard I of England undertake the Third Crusade.

1202–1204 — Fighters in the Fourth Crusade help Isaac Angelus recapture the Byzantine throne in Constantinople in present-day Turkey.

1217–1221 — Soldiers from Austria and Hungary launch the Fifth Crusade.

1228–1229 — Christians regain control of Jerusalem during the Sixth Crusade.

1248–1254 — King Louis IX of France leads the Seventh Crusade.

1270 — Louis IX leads the Eighth Crusade.

1271–1272 — The future King Edward I of England leads the ninth and last Crusade.

1337 — The Hundred Years' War begins between England and France.

1346 — England wins the important Battle of Crécy.

1453 — France defeats England in the Battle of Castillon, ending the Hundred Years' War. France recaptures most of its territories.

1488 — After nearly 200 years of existence, the most powerful version of the Swabian League forms in Germany.

October 31, 1517 — Martin Luther nails the 95 Theses to the door of the Castle Church in Wittenberg, Germany, launching the Protestant Reformation.

1524 — The Peasants' War of Germany begins.

1526 — The Swabian League defeats the peasants, ending the Peasants' War.

1534 — The religious split between Catholics and Protestants causes the Swabian League to dissolve.

1917 — King George V of Great Britain establishes the Most Excellent Order of the British Empire to knight people who have honored their country.

OTHER PATHS
TO EXPLORE

In this book, you've seen how the events surrounding the age of knighthood look different from three points of view.

Perspectives on history are as varied as the people who lived it. You can explore other paths on your own to learn more about what happened. Seeing history from many points of view is an important part of understanding it.

Here are some ideas for other knighthood points of view to explore:

+ A few women, such as Joan of Arc, fought as knights during the Middle Ages. What were their lives like?

+ Countries outside of Europe also had warriors similar to knights, such as Japan's samurai. How did their lives compare to those of European knights?

+ Many people learn about knighthood from the legends of King Arthur and the Knights of the Round Table. How were the lives of real knights different from these stories?

Read More

Gigliotti, Jim. *Knight Life*. Mankato, Minn.: Child's World, 2009.

Guillain, Charlotte. *Medieval Knights*. Chicago: Raintree, 2010.

Lassieur, Allison. *The Middle Ages: An Interactive History Adventure*. Mankato, Minn.: Capstone Press, 2010.

Murrell, Deborah Jane. *Knights and Armor*. Pleasantville, N.Y.: Gareth Stevens, 2009.

Internet Sites

FactHound offers a safe, fun way to find Internet sites related to this book. All of the sites on FactHound have been researched by our staff.

Here's all you do:

Visit *www.facthound.com*

FactHound will fetch the best sites for you!

GLOSSARY

bailiff (BAY-lif) — in medieval times, a representative of the lord who dealt with the peasants

chivalry (SHIV-uhl-ree) — a code of brave and polite behavior that knights were expected to follow

crusade (kroo-SADE) — a series of battles fought by European Christians in the Middle Ages to recapture land in the Middle East

hostage (HOSS-tij) — a person who is held against his or her will

jousting (JOUST-ing) — a sport performed on horseback with a lance

melee (MAY-lay) — a tournament involving many knights fighting at one time

peasant (PEZ-uhnt) — a person in Europe who worked on a farm or owned a small farm

serf (SURF) — a farm worker who was treated like a slave; serfs could buy their freedom.

siege (SEEJ) — an attack designed to surround a place and cut it off from supplies or help

trebuchet (treh-buh-SHET) — a weapon used to hurl rocks, liquid, or other items at an enemy

BIBLIOGRAPHY

Asbridge, Thomas. *The First Crusade: A New History.* New York: Oxford University Press, 2004.

Ayton, Andrew, and Philip Preston. *The Battle of Crécy, 1346.* Woodbridge, Suffolk, U.K.: Boydell Press, 2005.

Bax, E. Belfort. *The Peasants War in Germany, 1525–1526.* New York: Macmillan, 1899.

Blickle, Peter. *The Revolution of 1525: The German Peasants' War from a New Perspective.* Baltimore: Johns Hopkins University Press, 1981.

Bumke, Joachim. *The Concept of Knighthood in the Middle Ages.* New York: AMS Press, 1982.

The Columbia Encyclopedia. *"Knights Hospitaliers."* New York: Columbia University Press, 2008.

Riley-Smith, Jonathan. *The First Crusaders, 1095–1131.* Cambridge, U.K.: Cambridge University Press, 1997.

Saxtorph, Niels M. *Warriors and Weapons of Early Times.* New York: Macmillan, 1972.

Scaglione, Aldo. *Knights at Court: Courtliness, Chivalry, and Courtesy from Ottonian Germany to the Italian Renaissance.* Berkeley, Calif.: University of California Press, 1991.

INDEX